brave
this is us

A Catalytic Movement For Girls

Brave : This Is Us
Published by Orange, a division of The reThink Group, Inc.
5870 Charlotte Lane, Suite 300
Cumming, GA 30040 U.S.A.

The Orange logo is a registered trademark of The reThink Group, Inc. All rights reserved. Except for brief excerpts for review purposes, no part of this book may be reproduced or used in any form without written permission from the publisher.

Unless otherwise noted, scriptures taken from the Holy Bible, New International Version®, NIV®. Copyright © 1973, 1978, 1984, 2011 by Biblica, Inc.™ Used by permission of Zondervan. All rights reserved worldwide. www.zondervan.com The "NIV" and "New International Version" are trademarks registered in the United States Patent and Trademark Office by Biblica, Inc.™

Other Orange products are available online and direct from the publisher. Visit our website at www.WhatIsOrange.org for more resources like these.

ISBN: 978-1-63570-097-8
© 2019 Brave Global
Lead Writer: Cheryl Nembhard
Project Manager: Nate Brandt
Printed in the United States of America

First Edition 2019
3 4 5 6 7 8 9 10 11 12
10/30/20

This Is Us: Introduction

Hey, girl!! I'm so glad that you're here! I'm really looking forward to going on this journey with you, discussing life and all the things I've learned along the way about it! Life can be difficult when you don't have the answers for all the questions swirling around in your head. I know . . . I've been there. Our hope and prayer is that the words written here will give you peace of mind, confidence, hope, and a renewed sense of identity and will also challenge you to demand more of yourself—and for yourself.

As you read this book, I hope that your outlook on some things will change as you work through each chapter. Let this journal be a guide for you as you open your mind to the idea of healthy relationships between your friends, your body, your family, God, and yourself. Discuss it with those in your circles and hear their thoughts and stories about each topic as you do the activities we've composed to help you consider things in your life. At the end of the journal is a special section, created just for you to take some time and dig deeper into what you've read. If you're like me, you may need more space to unpack your thoughts, so for each chapter, there are corresponding pages at the back for you to continue your reflections. I encourage you to use them.

One of the biggest lessons I've learned is not to regret anything in life because EVERY experience teaches us something, which ultimately makes us better people. I always say that storms make the greatest teachers because they show us what we're made of and who is truly there for us, as well as the ways God moves in our lives. Open your mind to finding the lesson in everything. You will be amazed at how much life teaches you.

I'm so excited for each and every one of you!

In my mind, we're all having the biggest slumber party discussion ever . . . with our sisters from around the world! We're not holding back; we're going all in and talking about all of the things that matter to us right now. How awesome is this?

So, get comfortable, gather your friends, grab a snack, and let's dive in.

Let me share my life code with you. It gives me permission to be all that I was meant to be:
We will be **BOLD**, we will be **BRILLIANT**, and we will be **BRAVE**!

Why? Because the world needs what we have and because this is who we are!
THIS IS US!

With love,
Cheryl Nembhard

brave

[Chapter 1]
Brave Friendships

What makes someone a real friend?

> If you find someone who makes you laugh, who always tries to make you smile when you're down, who wants the very best for you, who cheers you on at all times, who loves you just the way you are don't let them go.
> Girl, those are "ride or dies."
> Good friends like that are hard to find.

What makes someone a real friend? What characteristics do they have? How should they treat you? Speak to you?

For so many years growing up, I didn't have the right answers to those questions and allowed some really horrible friends into my life. Because I didn't set a standard for myself and was just happy to have friends around, I ended up being used and betrayed. The wounds went deep and I promised myself that I would learn from those moments. From that time until now, what I look for in a friend has changed drastically. I don't just accept anyone into my life; I would rather have a few quality friends than tons of fake friends. Can you relate?

> Best friends are the people you can do anything and nothing with and still have the best time.

Crossword Puzzle

Good Friend List

Search for the qualities that you find in a good friend. Try to find the words listed below in this word search:

O	L	X	D	T	G	Y	N	N	N	D	A	N	R	W	G	G	L	Z	P	Y	S	O	Q	F	U	R	T	K	Y
E	P	N	X	J	E	X	H	D	I	U	X	D	U	P	G	N	E	A	J	D	P	F	T	A	Q	N	E	R	O
Q	I	N	V	S	T	U	N	T	O	T	K	D	V	M	W	N	I	N	Y	R	R	D	L	I	T	K	F	Q	B
K	Y	J	U	U	P	N	Q	S	R	Q	C	A	K	I	I	Y	I	N	E	O	T	K	V	T	F	W	V	M	L
U	J	H	G	E	C	R	U	T	Y	O	O	Z	K	J	C	P	F	G	E	R	L	O	Z	H	R	N	Z	S	S
T	L	G	R	P	A	K	T	Y	L	C	W	A	F	R	L	E	C	D	A	T	O	Y	X	F	D	Q	R	D	G
C	D	P	W	T	V	Q	O	M	O	Z	B	T	Q	A	N	F	M	I	P	R	S	U	N	U	Y	X	F	Y	F
G	N	I	V	I	G	R	O	F	P	Y	Q	U	S	L	U	Y	H	D	P	C	U	I	S	L	F	G	R	V	H
J	N	Y	H	Z	F	Q	L	E	A	N	C	H	B	U	G	T	A	V	P	P	P	O	L	S	N	G	L	X	U
C	H	O	W	E	H	X	R	I	H	I	V	N	F	P	R	G	H	K	M	Q	B	K	C	E	L	E	S	O	Q
V	J	Z	M	F	R	B	K	F	S	C	F	M	O	A	H	T	L	E	F	S	P	T	U	N	Q	A	B	N	A
S	U	P	P	O	R	T	I	V	E	E	N	S	E	D	W	W	R	J	N	N	H	K	V	G	E	H	H	V	W
Q	R	L	Y	V	E	D	N	P	R	O	T	E	C	T	I	V	E	G	J	T	G	L	N	D	O	D	G	Y	H
D	A	K	Y	B	W	R	E	S	P	E	C	T	F	U	L	O	T	H	J	L	I	I	W	N	S	D	H	K	E
L	T	Y	H	H	G	B	C	S	T	J	E	P	Z	E	H	A	U	A	E	Z	D	C	E	B	Y	Q	P	P	J
N	U	M	S	B	K	F	O	O	E	M	F	H	Z	C	L	Y	O	H	J	N	T	S	M	O	R	O	A	L	Y
O	A	F	P	B	S	F	H	G	F	N	C	B	I	U	Q	R	H	W	A	T	T	M	Q	S	Z	A	S	T	D
W	M	V	P	F	D	L	W	M	Z	Y	K	A	L	U	R	D	L	T	V	Y	P	M	H	C	R	Z	B	B	Z
K	P	D	A	L	Y	M	J	Z	B	I	Q	B	Q	N	R	L	S	K	W	U	U	P	V	N	A	U	S	R	G
B	I	S	W	K	E	U	Z	E	I	R	T	Z	U	D	D	R	N	G	U	J	T	F	G	F	T	T	J	Y	K
J	P	D	N	H	K	H	C	S	T	G	H	E	O	P	E	D	E	E	G	B	C	R	Z	P	S	G	E	E	L
W	G	R	F	Z	P	M	K	Z	M	U	Y	E	Q	D	D	V	X	L	C	Y	Z	I	T	D	F	X	U	H
J	R	V	F	P	F	V	L	K	S	V	I	R	N	I	Y	N	O	N	D	Q	I	C	T	Z	A	B	K	Y	R
T	I	D	M	S	U	D	P	C	R	M	Q	U	X	Q	R	F	E	D	N	S	M	Z	B	L	T	Y	A	Y	F
X	J	N	T	U	N	C	J	F	W	J	W	D	Y	Y	B	U	G	E	Y	Y	A	R	T	V	F	K	Y	N	Z
V	V	W	E	S	X	K	N	G	Y	P	A	S	C	A	P	N	A	G	E	K	E	T	C	S	S	I	G	V	A
Y	Z	G	E	G	B	E	G	Z	F	Z	C	R	N	C	X	X	D	N	C	V	M	L	S	K	C	F	Y	L	C
D	Q	E	Q	Q	E	W	X	U	S	G	W	T	O	X	X	C	K	U	I	Z	S	H	J	A	S	H	M	J	U
Z	Y	S	S	Q	C	D	A	D	R	M	C	U	A	U	N	Q	J	G	I	K	U	Q	M	H	H	D	G	C	V
Z	S	K	F	B	V	A	R	D	R	R	N	K	P	B	G	U	W	C	Q	H	O	M	F	R	O	K	Y	G	X

Advice	**Giver**	**Nice**
Authentic	**Helpful**	**Protective**
Encouraging	**Honesty**	**Respectful**
Faithful	**Kind**	**Supportive**
Forgiving	**Listening**	**Trustworth**
Generous	**Loyal**	**Understanding**

Friendship Journal

What other qualities are there? In your own words, tell me what a real friend means to you.

Fill in the blanks . . .

A real friend is

A real friend is

A real friend is

A real friend can

A real friend will

A real friend makes

A real friend makes

A real friend cares

A real friend doesn't

A real friend should

A real friend helps

How do we get more real friends?

So, what is the best way to get more real friends? The answer is simple: be a good friend to those around you. There's a cool proverb in the bible that says:"He that has a friend must first show himself friendly."

World-famous peace activist Mahatma Gandhi has a famous quote: "Be the change you wish to see in the world."

Be the friend you want to have. That means not putting on an act, being something that you're not, or pretending to be a certain type of person to attract friends. It's about you being more of the awesome person that you are and focusing on your good qualities. When it comes to being yourself, always be the real deal and keep it one hundred.

When we are our true selves, we will attract those who have similar interests and values.
That is where beautiful, genuine friendships are born. Here are some simple tips for making friends:

- It's okay to take the initiative in saying hello or hanging out
- It's good to expand your circle and meet new people
- Try not to take things too seriously or be too sensitive about things
- Don't give up after the first attempt, keep trying
- Be patient—friendships don't form overnight
- Take the time to get to know the person
- Don't force things; let friendships happen naturally
- Always **BE THE REAL YOU**

Reflection Journal

Brave Act

What parts of me do I want to see mirrored in those around me?

What parts of me do I need to shift or alter to be the best kind of friend?

What makes someone a bad friend?

Growing up as an only child, I struggled with feelings of loneliness. To fill some of those gaps, I would make my friends my family. They became my world and I would put their wants & needs above my own. Can any of you relate to that?

Needless to say, some of them took advantage of that; they abused my friendship and preyed on my insecurities. This type of bullying showed up in many ways: I always seemed to be the one to pay for stuff or they would borrow items from me and never give them back or wreck them, and I would always be the one to say, 'that's okay" or "you can pay me back whenever."

I always felt the need to do stuff for them so that they would like me. I felt like I was always the one giving and helping them with their stuff but would never get help when I needed it. Then there was the constant gossiping behind my back and knowing that they were talking badly about me whenever I wasn't there. I knew this was unhealthy but my thought was, "At least I have people to hang out with and I belong to a group."

Let me tell you, it's not worth it!
You are honestly better off on your own, working on yourself until the right friends come along (and they will).

If you're feeling used or devalued as a person consistently in any friendships, then it's time to take some space from those people. Let them know how their actions have affected you and that it's no longer acceptable for you to be treated this way.

Traits of a bad friend

Take some time and think about the people in your life that turned out not to be good friends:

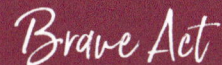

1. What makes someone a bad friend?

2. Describe the negative character traits that a bad friend could have and how they could affect you.

3. Is there someone in your life that you feel is not a good friend to you. Why? What steps are you going to take to correct that?

Frenemies

What is a "frenemy"? A frenemy is a person in your life (usually a so-called friend, someone in your circle, or a coworker) that you get along with and enjoy overall company but who will cut you down at virtually any opportunity with mostly backhanded compliments or digs about you. They root for you to do well—but not better than them. This normally stems from some jealousy they have of any, or all, aspects of your life. They can be similar to haters with whom you superficially get along).

There are different types of frenemies with different toxic behavioral patterns: from jealousy to backstabbing to those who try to control you. Whatever it is, you will know it because you don't feel good in that friendship. My advice is to be bold and speak honestly about how you're feeling and how their actions are affecting you & the friendship. If they continue with that same behavior, the next step is to take some space from that person.

> "Life is too short for fake butter or fake people. I would rather have an enemy who admits that they hate me, than a friend who secretly puts me down."
>
> **- KAREN SALMANSOHN -**

> "She's a jellyfisher: You have a conversation with her that seems all nice and friendly, then you suddenly feel like you've been stung and you don't know where it came from."
>
> **- HELEN FIELDING (BRIDGET JONES'S DIARY) -**

> "The friendships we keep can shape more than just the outcome of a situation, these individuals can actually shape who we are, and inevitably, who we become."
>
> **- ALEX AND ANI -**

brave

Chapter 2:
BOUNDARIES IN FRIENDSHIPS: WHEN TO SAY NO

Friendships are amazing. They're one of the most important relationships we form in life. When you have good friendships, it's the best feeling in the world. However, sometimes friendships can be draining; they can drain us of our joy, our peace, our power—and in worst cases, our voice. One of the most uncomfortable feelings is being in a relationship where you're feeling taken advantage of or abused. It's so important to set boundaries in our friendships to ensure that lines aren't crossed or that you feel like your thoughts and feelings are being considered.

3 Rules About Boundaries

1. **You are allowed to set boundaries to feel valued & safe**
2. **Anyone who wants to be in your life will respect your boundaries**
3. **You're allowed to walk away from anyone who doesn't respect them without apology**

People-pleasing

When it comes to friendships and boundaries, one of the things, we need to be careful of is "people-pleasing." People pleasing is a difficulty saying "NO" to other people's requests. It is someone who spends a great deal of time doing for others to be liked or accepted.

When to say no . . .

What are some of the ways that you've gone out of your way to please others?

How does that make you feel?

> Live your life for yourself, not others.
> Compromising to make others feel comfortable is never worth it.
> Being accepted or popular should never come with a price.
>
> - CHERYL NEMBHARD -

Effects of people-pleasing and the power of "no"

Do The Math

Pleasing Others
− **Your Own Thoughts & Feelings**
───────────────────
Losing your own identity

You lose who you are when you live a life to please others. It takes way too much energy to do what other people want you to do. You end up not being true to yourself.

GIRL LISTEN

The Power of No
One of the best ways to regain your power is the word "no." "No" can be your superpower. It has the potential to protect you from hurt & disappointment. Learn to say "no" more. It's okay to say "no."

What have been some of the reasons it's been difficult for you to say no in the past?

Brave Act

Who not to keep close

It's really important to evaluate your friendships from time to time to make sure they're serving you in a way that's healthy and not toxic.

Brave Act

Here's a checklist of types of friends to not keep close. Think about those in your life; are they like any of these?

Toxic Friends	What Are They Like	I Have Friends Like This
Emotional Vampires	People who drain you of your energy, your peace, your joy.	Yes or No
Guilt Trippers	Emotional Bullies who manipulate you by making you feel guilty for things	Yes or No
Gossip Girls	People who talk about others constantly in a gossiping way	Yes or No
Hype Haters	Those who have a problem when there's hype/buzz around you (e.g. success)	Yes or No
Cruel Comedians	People who say hurtful things (e.g. saying they're joking)	Yes or No
Just Jellies	Jealous of Accomplishments	Yes or No
Mean Makeover	People who try to change you always	Yes or No
Judge Judys	Friends who constantly judge everything about you	Yes or No

As you look at the list and think about all your friends, what comes to your mind?

_____

_____

_____

In a world where everything is up and down & you don't know who to trust at times, God is the only one who never changes. He is that one true friend who is always there for us.

> *Friends come and friends go, but a true friend sticks by you like family.*
> **- PROVERBS 18:24 (MSG) -**

Reclaiming your time

Reclaiming our time means refusing to waste any more time on people who take you for granted, abuse your kindness & friendship, and make you feel bad about yourself. It's time to choose to surround yourself with good & true friends.

Brave Act

Next to the clock below, write the characteristics/qualities you want the friends in your life to have.

1. _____
2. _____
3. _____
4. _____
5. _____
6. _____
7. _____
8. _____
9. _____
10. _____
11. _____
12. _____

Friendship circle

What does your friendship circle look like? Where do you place these types of friends in your life? In the circles below, place your friend group accordingly to how close they are to you.

School Friends
Work Friends
Best Friends
Acquaintances
Family Friends

Neighborhood Friends
Sports Team Friends
Church/Youth Group Friends
Other Friends

Different kinds of friendships are okay, too

Different types of relationships are okay.

Not everyone has to be your best friend, or even a close friend. Some friends will stay in your life for a very long time and some are only meant to be in your life for a season. Don't trip . . . people will drop off along the way and that's absolutely okay. For those that are currently in your life, there may be some that you'll get advice from. Some that you'll hang with from time to time, some that you'll only chill with at school or work, or someone you do everything with.

Brave Act

Are there friendships you're currently in that you don't feel comfortable with? List the reasons below:

You are in control of your feelings

Do people get you steaming mad?

Here's the tea:
No one has power over your emotions but you. People can work on your last nerve, but only you decide how you're going to react. The truth is that many of the people who hurt us are not worth our tears.

10 Tips to Take Control of Your Emotions

Always check in with yourself

Breathe, girl, breathe

Think before you speak

Take time away from the situation

Own your part in it

Pray about it

See the bigger picture

Ask: Is this worth my reaction?

Try to forgive & let go

Talk to a mentor about it

We teach people how to treat us

They say that actions speak louder than words. Nothing could be truer. It's the things we don't say and the things we allow that teach others what's acceptable behavior. If someone bosses you around, lies to you, manipulates you, or is mean to you—and has been for some time without any remorse—it's because you've shown them by your actions that they can and it's okay. Trust me, girl, I know this one stings, but I've got to keep it real with you.

Brave Act — Take some time and reflect on this life lesson and journal your thoughts.

I've taught people that it's okay to . . .

I've taught people that it's NOT okay to . . .

Now that we've learned about boundaries with our friends, what three boundaries do you feel would be healthy for you to set moving forward?

1. ------
2. ------
3. ------

brave

[Chapter 3]
ROMANTIC RELATIONSHIPS

Why do we want to have romantic relationships?

It's that thing that so many are obsessed with: romantic relationships.

We see them everywhere—like literally everywhere! They are all over social media, in all of our films & TV shows, plastered all over magazines and are over-fantasized in our novels. It seems like romance is the number-one topic: Who's dating who? Who's engaged to who? Who broke up with who? Don't get me wrong, romance is an awesome and wonderful thing to have. But it becomes harmful when we feel like we need to be in a romantic situation or something's missing from our lives. Why can't we be our own first crush? Why can't we be our own true love first? That special someone is supposed to be the icing on the cake that you're baking, not the actual cake itself!

Remember: Romantic relationships are wonderful things, but try not to lose yourself in them. Don't forget to live your life, too!

Media vs. real life

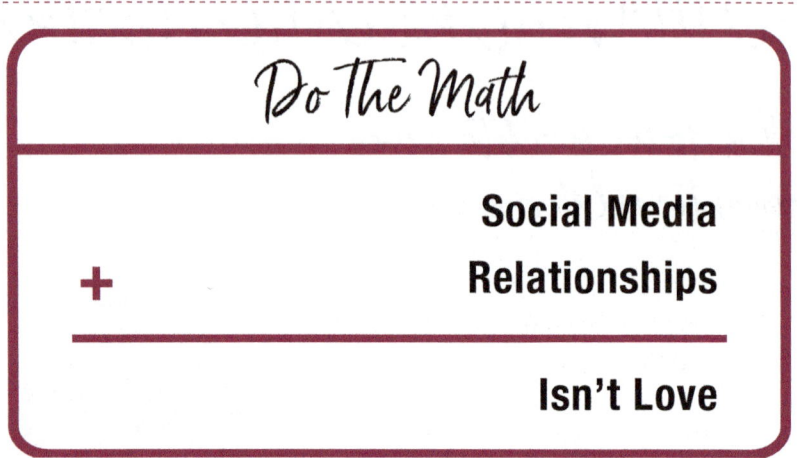

Do The Math

+ Social Media
  Relationships
  ———————
  Isn't Love

Honestly, the way we devour social media, shows, and gossip sites, you'd think that what we're seeing is real life! But, the truth is that it isn't. Just because we see stuff on our phones, tablets, and TVs doesn't make it real life, especially when it comes to relationships. The over-the-top-grand romantic gestures, the "baecations," the insta-worthy "picture-perfect" life seem ideal because the people look so shiny and happy in it! What happens behind the screen is actually the real indication.

Brave thought

One of the problems we face in relationships is having Hollywood-type expectations when it comes to dating. Let's face it, girls, not everyone is Michael B. Jordan! For those that are dating: be careful not to compare the person you're with to what you see in the media. Comparing can create tension in your relationship because the truth is they'll never be that other person. There's also feeling undue pressure to be in a relationship way before we're emotionally ready for one. We're given the messages that we're somehow incomplete without having someone in our lives. We think that finding "**THE ONE**" will make us whole.

> Girl, trust me, you don't need anyone—and I mean **ANYONE**—to make you whole or complete. **YOU ARE ENOUGH**!

What are the qualities we look for in a positive romantic relationship?

A lot of people can fall in love, but not everybody finds themselves in the healthy relationships they want. Why? Because we put so much focus on having a "bae" and being "boo'd up" and not enough energy in knowing what we're even looking for in a relationship.

So, what should we be looking for? I can tell you it's way more than any trashy lyric in a slow jam. It's way deeper than that. Here are my top-five qualities below. In the space below them, put your thoughts of why you think they're important, too.

Having strong trust between each other

Having happiness & laughter

Having respect

Having honest communication

Being supportive

Can you think of any other qualities that you would want in a positive romantic relationship?

What are the elements in negative romantic relationships we want to avoid?

Love can be many things, but there are a few things that love is not. The first, and most important one, is that love isn't abuse. Whether physical, emotional, or financial, abuse has no place in a relationship. No one has the right to hurt you, control you, or make you feel afraid—even if they say they do it because they love you.

Love shouldn't hurt.

Abuse almost always escalates. Often times, it starts out as emotional (name-calling, insults, controlling, intimidation, cruelty, etc.) and then becomes physical later. It doesn't matter how many excuses someone gives you, there is never a reason to allow abusive behavior. Remember, you are **VALUABLE**. No one should put their hands on you. It's absolutely wrong so you need to walk away . . . like now, hon.

#GetOut

Reflective Journaling

Has there ever been a time when you did not feel safe in a relationship? How did/does that make you feel?

Brave Act

ARE YOU CURRENTLY IN AN ABUSIVE SITUATION?
Want to talk about it with someone?
Call this helpline (toll-free): 1-800-799-7233

Self-esteem and confidence

> *"Why be YOU when I can be Me?"*
> **- CHERYL NEMBHARD -**

Have you ever seen a girl at school or even on the street where you're like, "Wow, I wish I had looked/could be like her?" Stop right there!

Listen, girl, as I said before, comparing is such an unhealthy thing to do. You being you is already good enough! The bible puts it this way in Psalms:

> *"I praise you because I am fearfully and wonderfully made; your works are wonderful, know that full well."*
> **- PSALM 139:14 (NIV) -**

Brave Act

Know that you are enough and that God made you just the way you are: beautiful. I know that self-esteem and confidence can be hard at times, especially when a lot of things out here are trying to bring you down. Sis, no matter what, you gotta keep your head up. Do you want to know why? Because you are a **QUEEN**! Yes, you! You're **ROYALTY**! You were created with a purpose, gifted with so many unique talents, and your future is super bright!

Always remember that!

Want some simple ways to help you gain that confidence?

1. **Mirror check:** Look into a mirror and tell yourself you are beautiful at least three times or until you actually feel it.

2. **Think positively:** Whenever you think a bad thought about yourself, apologize to yourself, then say something that you like about yourself.

3. **Stop comparing:** When you are about to compare yourself with someone, remember this and say it back: "I am my own person. I am who God made me to be. I am beautifully and wonderfully made!"

> **Try doing these three things whenever you think of yourself as "less than"**

Self-worth reflective moment

Write 5 things you like about yourself:

Draw yourself as a royal queen
(don't forget to add all the fun things like the crown, throne, and robe).

The "baewatch" word search

W	O	H	O	I	D	N	I	K	L	F	M	T	I	G	H	P	G	B	G
H	S	H	L	N	Y	T	I	L	I	B	A	R	E	N	L	U	V	K	W
Y	V	B	D	T	A	N	X	J	H	P	D	T	M	L	Y	E	C	Q	M
L	A	X	V	E	Q	F	E	C	B	Z	Q	Y	C	X	H	K	Q	A	Y
E	D	I	Q	L	Z	A	G	U	R	D	V	T	B	B	T	J	R	R	L
V	K	I	Z	L	C	N	N	H	M	E	M	I	Y	X	R	G	L	G	F
O	B	U	L	I	W	I	I	P	F	W	K	L	V	X	O	A	R	A	S
L	S	C	F	G	I	D	D	R	C	W	L	I	Y	V	W	J	E	K	U
R	O	R	H	E	N	H	N	E	Q	Z	E	B	M	I	T	N	W	D	O
B	V	U	I	N	K	Y	A	S	B	M	L	A	D	Z	S	Z	U	S	R
L	U	X	H	T	Q	L	T	P	I	R	A	T	D	C	U	O	I	T	E
U	E	Y	K	I	R	D	S	E	H	X	J	S	J	I	R	R	D	G	N
Y	Y	N	N	U	F	N	R	C	M	A	V	H	S	O	T	K	D	H	E
I	D	O	M	P	V	E	E	T	X	R	X	A	T	M	U	R	U	P	G
O	L	O	Y	A	L	I	D	F	E	V	I	T	R	O	P	P	U	S	J
O	J	E	M	J	V	R	N	U	L	Z	F	J	K	E	A	U	W	O	Y
H	W	C	D	Y	K	F	U	L	U	F	E	C	A	E	P	V	U	U	F
K	G	W	N	V	C	K	M	L	U	F	V	H	D	T	I	B	W	M	A
E	S	I	P	F	W	C	L	N	V	N	I	C	E	E	P	A	K	B	Y
V	U	A	S	W	J	B	W	G	F	X	P	H	M	J	Y	A	V	K	Z

Funny　　　　**Respectful**　　　**Kind**
Generous　　**Friendly**　　　　**Lovely**
Peaceful　　　**Intelligent**　　　**Nice**
Supportive　　**Loyal**　　　　　**Understanding**
Trustworthy　**Stability**　　　　**Vulnerability**

brave

Chapter 4:
SEXUAL WHOLENESS

Sex vs intimacy

S-E-X. Who knew that such a tiny, three-letter word, could have such a huge impact on our lives! There are so many questions, emotions, and thoughts around the subject that I thought we should spend a chapter looking at it, from a place of self-worth & value. That's really the place we should always approach sex from—valuing ourselves and our bodies.

When it comes to any sexual contact between two individuals, men and women are wired differently. For men, on the most part, it's viewed as a physical act. Because of that, men have the ability to approach sex without any deep emotional connections. Women, however, are not wired that way. In fact, for us, it's the complete opposite: we attach heavy emotions and thoughts to the act, which can cause us to be in a very fragile & vulnerable space, before or after making that decision.

Brave Act

How does self-worth & value play a role when it comes to sex?

Sex:
the physical act of sexual intercourse; sexual contact between individuals

Intimacy:
emotional closeness; a deep connection between two people

So many times, when we think of the term "intimacy," we mistakenly attribute it to a physical sexual context only. Believe it or not, physical or sexual contact is actually the lowest form of intimacy, behind relational, intellectual, and emotional intimacy (the highest form). Fancy words aside, the thinking that being sexual with someone will make you feel closer to them, safer, or more loved with your partner is actually . . . ta-da! Wrong. For anyone being pressured by someone to have sex for those reasons, just know that sex won't make someone love you. Also, if they're telling you that it's the only way to grow closer, they are lying. Period.

Sex without intimacy can look like some of the following scenarios: a one-night stand, sex without consent, an act which is paid for or sex as currency to get something else. Not really on your top-ten list, are they? For me neither.

Sex should be something very special, reserved for that person who is very, very special.

If I had my way, I would take every beautiful queen reading this now and lock them safely away in a tower until their "forever prince" came along and married them. Yup, just call me the "Disney Bodyguard," I'm fine with that. That's my dream. However, the reality is that some of you will become sexually active before marriage, so we want you to be safe, healthy, and informed to make the right choices.

Here's the horrible hook about hooking up

There's no denying, when you look around you, that we live in a "hook-up" culture. If you don't know what I mean by "hook-up," I mean casual sex. Unfortunately, casual sex is rampant in our society today. But here's the major problem with hooking up: casual sex is never casual.

Remember our discussion on intimacy, girl? Yeah, well because of the depth of intimacy involved for us as girls, in a sexual relationship, hooking up becomes not only difficult but damaging.

ARTS ACTIVITY & ANALOGY

Brave Act

WHAT YOU NEED:
2 pieces of different colored construction paper
1 bottle of glue
1 pack of pencil crayons
1 pair of scissors
2 of your favorite songs

WHAT YOU DO:
Cut the 2 pieces of construction paper in half (making 4 separate pieces). Take 2 pieces and lay them in front of you. Place some glue on one piece from the top to the bottom. Place the second piece on top of the glued paper and press down on both pieces together with downward strokes, from top to bottom, and then from left to right. Turn on your favorite song and create beautiful artwork on both sides for the length of the song.

Now separate the 2 pieces of paper, at normal speed. Repeat this same activity with one of the same papers, attaching it to a new piece of paper, using the same method and wait time.

What happened to the paper when you tried to separate it the first time? The second time? Describe the condition of the original paper now.

When we remove the papers after being glued together, it will leave behind a residue. The longer it remains, the more residue is left. You'll find that when you repeat this exercise, that paper will leave a residue wherever you stick it. What's interesting is that it will eventually lose its ability to stick to anything at all. This is what happens to us when we hook up randomly.

GIRL LISTEN

Each time we have a sexual encounter, we leave a part of ourselves behind. The longer the relationship goes on, the more we leave behind and the more we lose of ourselves. As we go from partner to partner, we lose so much of ourselves that we may eventually become numb inside and lose our ability to form any lasting sexual relationship at all. Sex no longer feels special and you start to feel damaged. Like that piece of paper.

Does waiting matter?

WORTH THE WAIT

I know that not all girls think the same or go through the same experiences, but I know that, at a certain age, we all start thinking about dating, love, and sex. True or false? For some of you, let's be honest, you can't wait for this particular chapter to be over just because this topic is so uncomfortable! That's OK.

For some of you, this chapter is really making you think twice about your value and maybe you feel like you have some decisions to make about your body and boundaries. If that's you, I'm super proud of you. We may be on different sides of the coin but no matter how you flip it, there is one question we all should be asking: Am I worth the wait? The answer is a no-brainer. Yes, you are absolutely worth the wait, and anyone that's with you should know that as well.

Let me ask you a question: If you have something that only you possess and people in your life kept asking for that thing, who would value it more? The person who got it right away or the person you made wait for it? Who would see that thing as more special? Exactly! There's something powerful about not just giving yourself away. Trust me, the moment you say "no" is the moment your stock goes up.

What am I waiting for?

Brave Act

You are a treasure and never forget it! In the space below write down things that you treasure most in your life:

No take-backs ...

Have you ever heard someone say that once you say something in the heat of anger, you can never take those words back? It's so true. I've lived my life by that code because I've seen the damage that comes when I just blurt stuff out without thinking. The sad thing is, even if the other person apologizes for all the things they've said to you when they were heated, it's still in the back of your mind, isn't it? Once it's out there, there's no taking it back.

If not having control over our words can cause damage sometimes, what about not having control over our own bodies? What level of damage can you cause yourself by not thinking things through when it comes to giving yourself to someone? Do you know of any situation where people deeply regretted being physical with someone? It's devastating—and I'm speaking from experience. You see, there was a time in my life when I was a teenager, that I was so broken & hurt, I just gave myself away to anyone. I thought that it would numb the pain inside. It only made it much worse. To be honest, it completely shattered me. Years later, I desperately wished I could take it all back.

Reason #282 of why you should wait?
Because in life, you can never go backward, only forward ...
and there are no take-backs.

The journey to YOU

> *I'm not perfect, but I know my worth. It took me a long time to find my crown. Now that I've found it, I will not accept anyone in my life who make me feel any less than the Queen I am.*
>
> **- CHERYL NEMBHARD -**

Brave Act

Sometimes in life, finding our worth is a difficult journey of a lot of ups and downs, decisions we wish we could take back, and learning from our mistakes. It may take a while, but once you find yourself, don't let anyone take that away. Imagine that **YOU** are at the center and this maze represents your life. Can you get to the core of **YOU**?

No means NO

Think about the words **"yes"** and **"no"** for a moment.

We've been saying those two words all our lives since childhood. As we grew up, we came to understand that they took on two very different meanings. "Yes" means to agree, to give permission, to approve. "No" means to disagree, to not give permission, to disapprove. Seems pretty straightforward, doesn't it? So why in the world would it be so difficult to understand the difference between yes and no when it comes to consent?

"Yes" and "no" are absolutes, there is no in-between. The excuses of being unsure, being led on, or not getting a clear answer from a partner are all bogus. If clear consent, in other words, permission is not given, then it's rape. Period.

I want you to know that no matter how friendly you are, what you're wearing, how fine you look, or whether you had a connection with that person, it still doesn't add up to a green light for anything you're not in agreement with. You hold all the power. You are in control. And no means no, period. Your consent must be clear, concise, and without any pressure added; anything else outside of that is a NO.

You have a voice. Don't lose it when it counts the most, girl. Speak up and speak out if you feel uncomfortable about any surroundings you find yourself in. Be super clear that consent has not been given—and then get away from that situation. As much as you can, travel with friends and be accountable for each other's well-being. Be on the lookout for one another. Don't leave each other behind.

Oh, and if you're with some idiot that doesn't seem to understand what no means, maybe they'll understand two other words: "BOY, BYE!"

brave

[Chapter 5]
VICTIM NO MORE

What is sexual abuse?

Sexual abuse, also referred to as molestation, is usually undesired sexual behavior by one person upon another. It is often perpetrated by using force or by taking advantage of another. When force is immediate, even if for a short duration, it's called sexual assault.

Sexual abuse is usually a term used in reference to minors. It occurs when an adult, adolescent, or older child uses a younger child or youth for his or her own sexual pleasure.

Sexual abuse can happen to both males and females, children and youths. It also includes "exploitation"—trafficking, prostitution, and child sex-abuse images (pornography).

Children or adolescents can be sexually abused by being touched in sexual parts of the body or by being forced to touch someone else's. Sexual abuse can also be non-touching.

My story

This chapter is a very personal one for me as I was sexually abused from the age of 5 to 12 years old. My abuser, like many abusers out there, was known to me—a so-called "friend" of the family. Their weapon was fear and they wielded it constantly. I can honestly say that it took over twenty years for me to be completely healed from it. The "how" for me is simple: I had to let God do it because I couldn't do it on my own. Through prayer, my church community, and counseling, I allowed God to remove each painful layer from me and toss it away. He's the greatest surgeon I know and He operated on my heart and my mind. You see, sexual-abuse survivors become like the zombies you see in horror movies: very dead inside. I was just a shell, completely numb and shut off to the world around me. I didn't care whether I lived or died, and I did everything I could to numb the pain, to shove it down further, including drugs, alcohol, violence, sex, on and off the streets. If you've experienced what I have, I would love to walk you through some things that really helped me.

GIRL LISTEN

Kids Help Phone: 1-800-668-6868

What to do if you've been sexually abused

The very first thing to do is to tell an adult that you trust, like a school counselor, your parent, your teacher/coach, a spiritual leader, or your uncle or aunt. If they don't take you seriously, try again. Keep speaking up until you get the help you need. In some cases, the abuser will threaten their victim with harm so they will stay silent. The truth is, once you speak up, the abuse gets exposed. By telling someone or calling the kids helpline (phone number above), the abuser will get caught and the nightmare will start to come to an end.

Know that it's **NOT YOUR FAULT**. In fact, it is **NEVER** your fault. Don't allow the guilt and shame to eat at you. You've done nothing wrong. Something very wrong was done to you.

Don't try to heal alone. There are professionals trained to help those who have been abused. Counselors are better equipped to help you work through your pain.

The effects of sexual abuse

For anyone who has experienced sexual abuse, the effects can be long-lasting into adulthood. As a survivor, here are some of the ways that sexual abuse affected me. Circle the ones that you identify with the most at this time:

Self-worth: Blaming yourself for the abuse. Feeling horrible about yourself. Thinking very low of yourself.

Anger: Unable to control your anger. Always having a temper and/or quick fuse.

Self-harm: Having thoughts of hurting yourself as a way of coping with painful thoughts and feelings.

Trust issues: Abuse can shatter your sense of trust in the relationships around you. Struggling with the overwhelming thought or feeling that no one can be trusted and that you're not safe. These feelings can cause you to isolate yourself.

Disconnection: This is when you disconnect yourself from the events of your past. You separate from them until you have a hard time remembering them or feel like you're just going through the motions and nothing around you is real.

Your voice matters

Ladies, gather around and let me tell you something. Your voice is one of the most important instruments in your body. Your voice can instantly change your situation. Always speak up for your safety, your comfort, and your standards. I wish you could get a glimpse into the future of how powerful your voice will be. Your  voice can reach millions. Your voice can create businesses out of thin air. Your voice can raise issues about things that occur all over the world or even in your local community. Your voice can and will do wonders! Never be silent because others tell you to. Your voice is your power! You will not be silenced! A great poet, Audre Lorde in her book called "The Black Unicorn: Poems" said, ". . . When we speak, we are afraid our words will not be heard nor welcomed, but when we are silent we are still afraid, so it is better to speak . . ."

Use the voice God gave you and speak your mind because whatever you put your mind to, you can achieve!

Affirmations

Brave Act

Below, fill in the blanks of all the amazing things that your voice is and will do. Even if you don't feel it right now, write down the things you would love to believe about your own voice (example: "My voice is powerful," "My voice will change the world," etc.)

My Voice _____
My Voice _____
My Voice _____
My Voice _____
My Voice _____

Self-defense moves

"Don't underestimate learning self defense!

Self defense begins with using your voice and making your **"NO!"** known when you feel unsafe. Every girl would benefit from also knowing basic physical self defense moves. Find a local class in your community that offers this training so you can feel prepared for anything. You were made strong and worth fighting for - why not empower yourself to be the safest you can be?!"

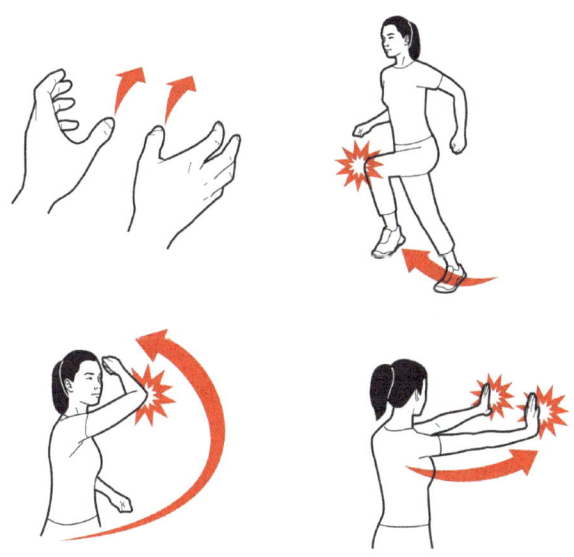

https://www.thehealthy.com/

Breathe... You are victorious!

Before you read this, I want you to breathe because sometimes we can forget.

Inhale. Now exhale . . . Listen to me, all is not lost and your life isn't over. Inhale again. Now exhale. Breathing is always important because when we're stressed out, we forget to breathe sometimes.

I want you to know that all of the problems and situations you may be facing right now will pass. I guarantee you that they will not stay forever. It feels like they will, but trust me, they don't. So that's why we can't keep our minds stuck on situations, because they won't stay like that forever. Trust me, the problems you think are huge right now, like being in elementary/middle school or even high school, won't matter once you're out. All those things you've done and mistakes you've made do not define who you are, so don't ever let them stop you from being and doing what you're called to do! More importantly, God is with you. You are never alone. And with God on your side, you win! One of the dopest verses in the bible is from Romans 8:31 which says,

> "If God is for me, who can be against me?"

For real, God's on your side!

brave

[Chapter 6]
OUR RELATIONSHIP WITH OURSELVES

Who are you in the grand scheme?

Here's the thing about Identity: once you are grounded in yours, everything changes. It's so important to know who you truly are, not what society or the media says about you.

Self-perception (how you see yourself), affects our actions and the way in which we exist in the world. Here's an easy equation to help you remember this:

HOW I SEE MYSELF = HOW I CARRY MYSELF.
(e.g., seeing myself as a queen – carrying myself as a queen)

Seeking affirmation from others in your life can be both misleading and destructive. Allowing your friends, frenemies, or social media to tell you who you are really isn't the way to go. I always say, if you want to know the true design or function of something, you have to seek the creator of it.

Know that you are beautiful, inside and out. You are a unique creation, made for a purpose . . . on purpose! Nothing about you is an accident. You have a destiny, and the best part is—you have your whole life to discover it!

Personal inventory

Here's a cool personality test to take for yourself!

Brave Act

It's a fun exercise that will hopefully give you more insight into how beautifully unique you've been made!

Take some time to reflect as you think about your answers. If we all take the time to check in with ourselves, we'll come to realize that we know more about ourselves than we actually thought.

Circle your answers to the following 20 sentences.
Agree or Disagree (Agree = 2 points, Disagree = 0 points)

You enjoy loud parties with lots of people.	Agree or Disagree
You love spending time fantasizing about unrealistic ideas.	Agree or Disagree
You think about what you should've said in conversations.	Agree or Disagree
Your first instinct is to support someone or fix their problem.	Agree or Disagree
People rarely make you upset.	Agree or Disagree
You depend on other people to start conversations.	Agree or Disagree
You care what people think of you after you meet them.	Agree or Disagree

When you spend time with yourself, you feel bored.	Agree or Disagree
You're more into the details than the big picture.	Agree or Disagree
You're very affectionate with people you care about.	Agree or Disagree
You're bothered by the mistakes you made in the past.	Agree or Disagree
At parties, you keep to yourself.	Agree or Disagree
You can stay calm under pressure.	Agree or Disagree
You don't mind crying in front of others.	Agree or Disagree
You make decisions with your heart rather than your head.	Agree or Disagree
You prefer to get revenge rather than forgive.	Agree or Disagree
Your emotions control you more than you control them.	Agree or Disagree
You always consider how your actions affect others.	Agree or Disagree
You rarely feel insecure.	Agree or Disagree
You always make careful, well-thought-out decisions.	Agree or Disagree

SCORE = _ _ _ _ _ _ _ _ _ _ _ _

Brave girls personality test results

Score 28–40: extrovert, intuitive, feeling dreamer, assertive

Score 0–20: introvert, observant, thinking, loyal, unwavering

Score 22–26: extrovert/introvert combo:
a unique balance of both qualities

Score 28–40:
You can change the world with just one idea! You are a visionary who is curious about new things and ideas. You are fiercely independent and you crave creativity and freedom over stability and security. When you find a cause that sparks your imagination, you are ignited. The energy that you bring to that cause or project throws you into the spotlight. You are very observant and a good judge of character. You are enthusiastic, friendly, and a natural-born leader. You think more in terms of the big picture than finer details. When you love, you love hard. You can't help being the life of the party and tend to stand out in whatever setting you are in.

Score 0–20:
You are a person of integrity and loyalty. You are a person who keeps their word and does exactly what they say they'll do. When you make a decision, you stick to it. You are very trustworthy. Because you are the dependable one, you are sometimes left to take up the slack. Honesty is a priority for you, and sometimes you can come across as blunt as a result of that. You are a facts person and like to hear both sides of the story. You're not a fan of conflict, manipulation, or mind games. You like to keep to yourself and enjoy being on your own with your own thoughts. For the most part, you are calm, practical, and grounded.

Be B.R.A.V.E. "B"

BE BRAVE

"B" = Be Bold

Be bold! Be bold in everything you do, girls. Never hold back in showing people who you really are. You are beautifully and wonderfully created by God. Never forget that, girl!
You are greater than you know; you are stronger than you know. Be bold with every problem you face. For example, if you find yourself being treated badly or seeing someone being treated badly but haven't spoken up about it, that's not being bold. Always speak your truth because no one else will do it for you.

Be bold in every way possible.

That could mean many things like being bold in your beliefs, your morals (what you will and will not do), bold in your fashion, bold in your attitude, and so much more.

Being brave is your superpower . . . and boldness is your weapon!

However, making the choice to be bold can take time because there's always a part of us that's hesitant or worried about what could happen. I truly understand that feeling, but I want you to know that when you show up fully as your authentic self, without apology, it is life-changing. Right at that moment, you arrive at that amazing point where you no longer care what other people think or say about you. I call it "being allergic to people's opinions."

When you're ready, there's a verse in the bible that really encourages us to take that bold leap:

> "God did not give you the spirit of fear but love, power and a sound mind"
>
> **- 2 TIMOTHY 1:7 -**

So be bold, girl! And don't let that crown fall.

> "Be Bold. Be Brilliant. Be Brave. The world is waiting for all that you are."
>
> **- CHERYL NEMBHARD -**

Be B.R.A.V.E. "R"

BE BRAVE

"R" = Be Resourceful

Resourcefulness is one of the most important traits you can possess in life. Someone who is resourceful will have the mind-set that "there is always a way." Resourceful people are out-of-the-box thinkers who don't give up. When you're faced with a challenge, instead of retreating away, dig deep and ask yourself, "How can I make this work?" Be open-minded and willing to try new approaches to things. Believe that you have the ability, skill, and bravery to handle any challenge.

Your first feeling may be that "it's too hard" or "I can't do it."

Are you kidding? You're a **GIRL BOSS**! You got this!

Being resourceful also means looking at what's in front of you or what you've been given and making the most of it. When I was growing up, my mom and I struggled financially and I didn't have the best clothes. In the beginning, I got teased about it, but then I decided to use the strength I've relied on my whole life: my creativity. Girl, I cut, colored, and folded up my outfits and made them fashion!

Don't give up because it seems hard. Dig deep and be creative. You will be absolutely blown away with what you come up with.

> *"Do what you can, where you are, with what you have!"*
> **- TEDDY ROOSEVELT -**

Be B.R.A.V.E.

Brave Act

How are you going to be braver?

How are you going to be more resourceful?

Be B.R.A.V.E. "A"

BE BRAVE

"A" = Be Adaptive

Adapting is not always easy, but, girl, it's so important in life.

Being adaptable means being able to adjust to new conditions. Here's what I know for sure: change isn't something we like all the time. However, I've learned that change is good for us. We grow from change; we learn from change. So, even though being adaptable can be a bit hard, adapting can truly be rewarding in the end.

Being adaptable also means going with the flow. We can't always have everything structured or planned out the way we want it to go, because life doesn't work like that. I've learned in this life that God doesn't move or flow with what works for us in our schedule. We move through His. No matter how many times I try to structure and plan my outcome, it never quite goes the way I planned, and I end up disappointed or frustrated.

Imagine our lives as one huge book written from beginning to end. I find that when I let God write my chapter, it's way better than anything I could've done myself. God's plan for us is better than the one we can imagine

People ask me constantly how I got to where I am now. Simply, I learned to put my pen down and stop trying to write my own story.

God's version has been the absolute greatest adventure! So, don't take it personally when things don't go your way. Sometimes the delay is for your good or because something better is coming. Learn to be flexible with where life is going and what changes it can bring. Yes, it may seem unknown and scary, but know that you're never alone—God's got you! One of the coolest things I heard was "one plus God will always be the majority."

Repeat it with me:

SOMETIMES CHANGE IS A GOOD THING.
I WILL LEARN TO BE ADAPTABLE.

> "I know what I'm doing. I have it all planned out—plans to take care of you, not abandon you, plans to give you the future you hope for."
> - JEREMIAH 29:11 (MSG) -

Be B.R.A.V.E. "V"

BE BRAVE

"V" = Be Victorious

Nobody wants to live a defeated life. Yet, there are moments in our lives when things hit us really hard and we find ourselves feeling pretty crushed and defeated. My prayer for you is that you will be victorious in this life; for some, that might mean a change in mindset.

Being victorious means living as if you've got the victory. To have the victory means to win.

One of the first steps I took to living a victorious life was switching my mentality from "victim" to "victor." What do I mean by that? A victim mentality simply means that you're living constantly in this prison of "why me" or "poor me" all the time. My feelings of being used and abused all my life, like trash, were taking control of me. I felt powerless. The more I drowned myself into those feelings, darker feelings, like depression and suicidal thoughts, entered my mind and soul as well.

Defeat looks like shame, guilt, and hatred of self. Those three became my worst "frenemies" and they wouldn't leave me alone. My life completely changed when someone who was filled with the love of God told me what I'm about to tell you: this dark moment that you're in is NOT the end of your story. There's so much more ahead; your story is just being written. In fact, there is a brand-new chapter, a fresh start, a "do-over" waiting for you . . . that is, if you want it.

Victory looks like daily prayer, regaining your power, self-love, self-confidence, a winning mindset, joy, and forgiveness. My hope is that you'll get to a place where you can experience all of the above, fully and freely.

Be B.R.A.V.E.

Brave Act

How are you going to be more adaptable?

How are you going to victorious?

Be B.R.A.V.E. "E"

BE BRAVE

E = Be Enough

What does it mean to be enough?

Being enough is being satisfied with who you are and not changing for anyone. You are enough because you don't need to be anything or anyone else to please others. You are enough because just being yourself is beautiful and amazing and perfect, all at the same time. The world tells you that you need to be more, do more, and that you can never measure up.

That's all a lie! Actually, it's more like a trap.

The truth is that the world needs more people to be their unique, different, quirky selves, and we are better when we have all of this amazing variety around us.

We're all searching to be loved, cared for, and protected. Everyone deserves that right. However, there's a big difference between searching for love and searching for validation from others. Every new morning that we're given on this earth to wake up and breathe is a morning that God has already made you enough. I gotta say it again: you're already enough, girl. You didn't have to do anything more to get there. Like Beyoncé says, "You woke up flawless."

God is perfect and he made us in his image, so he made no mistake when he made **YOU**!

Whenever you're feeling sad or anxious about not feeling like you're enough, just know you are loved because God IS love. Whenever you feel down about yourself, I want you to look in the mirror and tell yourself you are enough as many times until you feel that you really are. We're queens and we NEVER let that crown fall because we have way too much to offer the world. Don't let people tell you who you are and that you're not enough. God says that you are. Period. It's time to start being allergic to people's opinions of you (wink).

Make an acronym with your first & last name using positive words of affirmation
(ex: CHERYL = Confident, Honest, Enthusiastic, Real, Youthful, Leader)

Brave Act

What are you passionate about?
What could you see yourself doing or being a part of for the rest of your life?

brave

Chapter 7
SELF-CARE IS NOT STUPID

Yeah . . . so basically when I was growing up, I had a superhero complex. What do I mean by that? I thought that I didn't need help from anyone for anything. I hustled my way through life and I had a "survivor's" mentality (no space to dream, don't let your guard down, don't allow yourself to feel, etc.). Back then, when people mentioned the idea of self-care to me, I would laugh until my eyes watered. Of course, that would be followed up with my best high-pitched sarcastic voice asking if "I was too late for my spa appointment." "Did my nutritionist show up with lunch?" or "When would Fabio have my massage room ready?" That would have those around me cracking up. I always had a way of making people laugh. I was the life of the party, wherever I went.

Except, I was using laughter to cover up what was really going on with me.

You see, I was emotionally and mentally a mess inside. There was a constant storm of pain and anger that permanently raged inside of me. My body carried a lot of my past trauma, and I lived in constant stress. I wasn't making the connection that what I was carrying was affecting how I was living. I wasn't sleeping properly, or at all. I was an emotional eater (which means I basically ate my feelings). I wasn't making the best choices for my body (doing drugs, alcohol, no water, non-stop all-nighters, etc.). I was pushing myself to the point of exhaustion and I was extremely self-hating. That combo proved to be nearly fatal, with several emergency trips to the hospital.

I finally figured out two things: I was human after all . . . and self-care is not stupid.

Self-care is not a fluffy word, it's crucial to our well-being. The sooner we figure that out, the better it is for us. When we focus on self-care, we are able to be a better daughter, sister, friend, mother, and girlfriend to others.

In the next few pages, I want us to take some time to talk about what self-care looks like for the mind, body, and soul.

> "Self-care is never a selfish act. It is simply good stewardship of the only gift I have, the gift I was put on earth to offer others. Anytime we can listen to true self and give the care it requires, we do it not only for ourselves but for the many others whose lives we will touch."
>
> **- PARKER PALMER -**

Mind: self-talk

There's a beautiful scripture in the bible that says that we are to "love others as ourselves." As I live out my faith over the years, I've really held on to that verse as a guide to loving those around me well. As a social-justice advocate, it's always been one of my anchor verses. It wasn't until recently that I realized I was only looking at that verse from one angle and missing a very important aspect.

Let me put it this way . . .

I just love how DJ Khaled is always talking about "giving the keys" of life! Well, here's a big "key" for you: we're supposed to love ourselves well. Loving ourselves is a huge part of our freedom! In fact, we should be our own first love.

We should learn to love ourselves first instead of desperately waiting around for other people to love us. One of the first orders of business to loving ourselves well is to be kind to ourselves. I have to say it again: you have to be kinder to yourself, hon.

I know that might sound easy to some, but it might be difficult for many of you who are reading this. This is an important conversation that needs to be had. If we are not kind to ourselves, how can we expect others to be kind to us? We must be gentle with what we think about ourselves. The truth is, we can be our own worst enemies. If this is you, I want you to promise me that you will stop beating yourself up with horrible thoughts about yourself.

Those thoughts that are not true can cause so much damage.

Not only must we be kind with what we think about ourselves, but also be kind in what we say to ourselves. There's a verse in the bible (Proverbs 18:21) where it says that *"life and death are in the power of the tongue."* Wow, think about that for a moment . . . life and death.

Think about how many times you've called yourself fat, stupid, lazy, or ugly. If we're saying cruel things like that about ourselves, we're killing our self-esteem, our confidence, our joy, and our peace of mind. When God created you, He made a masterpiece, and that's exactly how He sees you!

So, challenge yourself to always speak life-affirming words to yourself. Be your own cheerleader and don't wait for anyone else to pick up those pom-poms for you!!

Brave act: self-talk exercise & vow

> *"Love yourself first, because that's who you'll be spending the rest of your life with."*
>
> **- ANONYMOUS -**

Take some time and think about your awesomeness!

Brave Act

Name 7 things that you love about yourself:

1. _____
2. _____
3. _____
4. _____
5. _____
6. _____
7. _____

Our brave promise

Today is a brand new day.

The days of being our own worst enemy are behind us.

Today we renew our minds and the ways we've thought and spoken about ourselves.

Today we put an end to the destructive self-talk & negative thinking.

Today we make a promise to love ourselves well.

Repeat after me . . .

I promise not to beat myself up over the mistakes of my past.
Instead, I will

I promise to no longer say horrible things about myself.
Instead, I will

I promise not to hold on to friends that are
toxic, hurtful, stressful, or jealous.
Instead, I will

I promise not to hold on to negative thoughts and feelings about myself.
Instead I will

I promise to be kinder to myself and to give myself the same love, care, and support I would give to anyone else.

Signed _____

Dated _____

Mind: counseling

If you find yourself going through a traumatic time right now or working through overwhelming feelings from a traumatic past, one of the greatest gifts you can give yourself is counseling.

You know, just writing that sentence for me is so huge because of the social hurdles I had to jump over to finally appreciate the benefits of going to a counselor. Growing up in my community, you didn't dare mention the word "therapist." It was frowned upon and seen as a waste of time and money.

No matter how bruised we were, we had to keep our feelings to ourselves and pray through it. Sharing our feelings with strangers was considered weak, and receiving guidance from them meant that we lacked faith that God would work it out.

The social stigma against seeking help has ended up hurting us on a far deeper level than we could imagine. As Oprah always says, "Here's what I know for sure:"

Going to a counselor is actually a sign of strength. It takes an incredibly strong person to say that they need help.
Going to counseling is not a faith issue. Prayer is powerful and it changes things. Having someone to talk to and work through your feelings is also a direct answer to your prayers that your situation gets better.

Counseling provides a much-needed place of safety, with no judgments. Many of us can't find that space with our family or friends. In some cases, it's better speaking to someone who has an outside perspective.

They are trained professionals who can help you sort through your feelings in a skilled way without making you more upset about your situation.

It works. Period.

Mind: resources

One of the best ways to clear your mind and get into the right space is to talk with someone about the issue. You can talk to a parent and/or guardian, a friend, or a family member that you're close to. If you find that you need something more, then it might be a good idea to seek out a counselor at your school or community program.

However, if you're a bit too scared to do that in person, here are some links to websites & numbers that can help you get on the road to recovery:

www.teenmentalhealth.org

www.walkalong.ca

www.goodtherapy.org

www.counselling.org

https://www.rainn.org/get-help

National Suicide Prevention Hotline: 1-800-273-8255

www.iprevail.com

www.nafcclinics.org

A Safe Place: 1-888-290-7233

Kids Help Phone: 1-800-668-6868

https://www.samhsa.gov

Body: diets suck

We were born to be real,
Not to be perfect.

Can I just help some of my incredible, brave girls right off the top?

This goes out to every dope queen who's reading this and struggles in this area: please stop calling yourself fat and PLEASE stop punishing your body by putting it through diet after diet!

Why? Honestly, because diets suck, that's why.

The diet industry is a multibillion-dollar business designed to play on our insecurities about our own body. We see it everywhere: the tremendous pressure to have the "perfect body" is all around us.

But what is that anyway? Who defines that? The flood of images and videos showing "flat- tummy teas," diet pills, hunger-suppressing gummy bears, or skinny-gal shakes is absolutely overwhelming. Dieting is literally prescribed to everyone, at all times, in every magazine you read.

Dieting is like a hamster running on its wheel: once you get on, it just never ends! Before you know it, you're spending your entire life chasing some magical number and starving yourself constantly while missing out on really important things like healthy eating habits and exercise.

Get this: the US National Library of Medicine states that after just one year, dieters ended up gaining back 30–60% of the weight they were trying to lose. Sis, forget the starving. Stick to healthy eating and exercise.

Body: healthy eating

After drinking my bodyweight in SlimFast shakes, I realized that I was completely barking up the wrong tree when it came to looking and feeling my best. Honestly, guys, there's no quick fix or magic pill or diet. You can stop searching. The answer is simple: it's what you put in your body. Girl, listen, healthy eating is **EVERYTHING**.

Here's a food guide that can make a huge difference in your life, from girlshealth.gov:

Fruits and vegetables are packed with vitamins and minerals. They also have fiber which helps you feel full and is great for you. Try to fill half your plate with a variety of different fruits and veggies. And instead of drinking juice, try to munch on whole fruits, whether frozen, canned, or dried.

Whole grains have lots of health benefits, including possibly helping prevent heart disease. At least half your grains should be whole grains. This includes whole wheat, oatmeal, and brown rice. (It even includes popcorn—just watch out for added butter and salt.) Fat-free and low-fat milk products are great. They are especially good for a girl during her childhood and teen years because she needs them to build strong bones. Look for fat-free or low-fat cheese, yogurt, and other dairy products. If you can't drink milk, try soy drinks fortified with calcium and vitamin D.

Protein helps your body heal, gives you energy, and more. Choose a mix of different protein foods. Good options include fish and other seafood, poultry (without the skin), lean meats, beans and peas, eggs, soy products, and unsalted nuts and seeds. Try to pick fish and shellfish in place of some meat and poultry.

Foods to limit. Some foods are not good for your health if you eat too much of them. Try to have less of these:

Solid fats, which are fats that are solid at room temperature. Solid fats are usually high in saturated fat and trans fat, and eating too much of them can cause problems like heart disease. Oils that have unsaturated fat are a much healthier choice (e.g., olive oil, coconut oil, canola oil).

Sodium is found in table salt and also in lots of prepared foods. Eating too much sodium can cause health problems, such as high blood pressure.

Added sugars mean you're getting extra calories without any extra nutrients. Added sugars are often hiding out in your soda, cookies, candy, and sugary cereals.

Refined grains are grains that have had some of the nutrients removed. Choose whole grains because they have more of the nutrients.

Cholesterol can increase your risk of heart disease. Check the Nutrition Facts labels on foods you eat to see how much cholesterol they have. Try to eat as little cholesterol as possible. Cholesterol usually comes from foods like ice cream, steak, and other animal products.

> "I can't control everything in my life, but I can control what I put in my body."
>
> **- ANONYMOUS -**

Soul: prayer & meditation

Now that we've walked through what self-care looks like in our mind and body, let's take a minute and talk about feeding our souls. I think the simplest way to define the soul would be the "spirit" or "essence" of a person. It's that immaterial part of us where our emotional and intellectual energy lies. This quote from Pierre Teilhard de Chardin really sums it up for me:

> "We are not human beings having a spiritual experience. We are spiritual beings having a human experience."
> - PIERRE TEILHARD DE CHARDIN -

Our soul is the place where we connect with God, our Creator. The bible says that our souls are the most valuable things we have; more than anything we can have or do in this world. There's a powerful verse found in Matthew 16:26 that says: "What good will it be for someone to gain the whole world, yet lose their soul? Or what can anyone give in exchange for their soul?" Wow, pretty heavy, right? Our souls are valuable to us, but more importantly to God. He cares about the condition of our souls.

It's so important that we do things that feed our souls and that strengthen our inner being.
Two of the biggest, most fulfilling things are prayer and meditation.

What is prayer anyway? Sometimes the idea of it can be so mystical and mysterious. Here's the simplest way to think of prayer: prayer is just having a conversation between you and God. That's all.

And just like so many conversations in life, you can talk about how you're feeling, what's going on with you (good or bad), what you need help with, or what you're hoping can be done in a situation — anything at all. God cares about all of it! He cares deeply about you and what you're feeling.

So, if prayer is simply talking with God, then meditation would be listening.

Meditation is the act of quieting the mind and being still. I personally love to just have a moment of silence before or after I pray. When you think about it, what kind of one-sided relationship would it be if someone only talked at you all the time and never let you say a word in response? Crazy, right? I laugh just thinking about it! Sometimes, it's in that silence that the answers, instructions, and next steps you've been waiting on come to you clearly.

You don't need a fancy church to pray. Prayer can be wherever you are, at any time. And when you can't put your prayer into words, it's okay, God hears your heart.

brave

Chapter 8
This Is Us
Body Positivity

Puberty

Okay, so here's the moment when you may squirm a bit.

If you're like me, then you can probably discuss hair, make-up and clothing nonstop for days. Those are some of our favorite topics, am I right girls?

However, the moment I bring up the words "period"' and "puberty," you're probably going to want to excuse yourself for an extended bathroom break and put the journal reading on pause! I get it... but please keep reading. I fully understand how the topic of our changing bodies is never one that we want to run to in discussion. But the truth of the matter is, puberty is coming or has come and is drastically changing our bodies, so let's talk about it!

During puberty, your body will grow faster than any other time in your life. It's also during that time that you may feel like no one understands what you're experiencing. Honestly, every single one of us has gone through it. Relax, you're not alone.

Puberty for girls, starts somewhere between the age of 8 and 13 yrs old. Some people start puberty a bit later than that time as well. Each person is unique, so they will start and go through puberty on his or her body's own schedule. This is one of the reasons why some of your friends might still look like kids and others look like adults. Our bodies get curvier and our breasts start to grow. It is absolutely normal during puberty to experience weight gain. Natural weight gain is all part of your body changing shape.

Another noticeable sign that you are going through puberty would be hair growth. I wish we were talking about a 'Rapunzel' situation, but we're not. I'm talking about hair growing under your arms and on your private parts. Yes, I said private parts...just breathe.

It's super duper important during this time that you stay on top of your hygiene because the combination of hair and puberty hormones will result in a stronger odor than normal.
Again, all very natural and part of the process.

Periods

Another big change during puberty is that you begin ovulating, which means that your body becomes capable of becoming pregnant. Every month your body will go through an ovulation cycle that causes extra blood and tissue to be stored in the womb in the event of pregnancy. When pregnancy doesn't occur, everything that was stored up then releases, making up your period. A period cycle lasts between 5-7 days and is anywhere from 25-35 days apart.

To absorb menstruation flow, you have two choices: sanitary napkins (pads) or tampons. Pads are external while tampons are used internally. Pads should be changed often before they're completely filled up or it may soak through to your clothing - nobody wants that. Tampons need to be changed every 4 hours or less. Leaving your tampon in longer than that can put you at risk for **Toxic Shock Syndrome (TSS)**, which is a rare but potentially deadly disease.

Just before your cycle, you will notice that you may have emotional mood swings or that your body is experiencing bloating, cramps or acne. This is called PMS (pre-menstrual syndrome) and it can make a grown woman be reduced to a Netflix-binging, ice cream & chocolate eating, bag of emotions! Good news: the symptoms go away after the first few days of a period.

When it comes to cramps, they can get pretty severe for some girls. I recommend a warm heating pad/bottle for your stomach and midol or ibuprofen for the pain.

Here's a cool way of looking at the whole period thing:
Once a month your 'friend' will come to visit you, it more than likely will be slumber party for part of it. Bring snacks, pain relief, a good movie & something to read (wink).

> "Why Period Cramps? Can't my Uterus just text me and be like 'what's good girl, so you're not pregnant. Love you, see you next month."
>
> **- ANONYMOUS -**

Being Comfortable in Your Own Skin

I want you to do me a favor,
my brave warrior girl.

Although it's a favor that I'm asking of you, this favor is really for you. It's going to protect your heart, set you free, and help you grow confidently in your own skin. Here it is: I want you to develop a severe allergy for me. One so severe that you can't be around the irritant whatsoever...if you even begin to sense it, you get affected.

I want you to become allergic to negativity, in all forms.

That means negative opinions of you, negative/hurtful words said to you, gossip, back-biting, constant complainers...you get the picture. I want you to live day-to-day from a place of JOY not HAPPINESS. There's a huge difference.

If Happiness is being on a big yacht on a beautiful day, then Joy would be the anchor that holds that ship steady & unmoveable in times of storms. Happiness comes and goes. Joy goes deeper.

The joy in maturing and becoming more comfortable in your own skin happens when your happiness is not connected to what people think or say about you. If I could fill your closet with t-shirts, they would say things like:

"I'm allergic to gossip."

"I'm sorry, I don't do negativity."

"If it's not positive, keep it moving."

"Negativity makes me itch."

etc.

You see where I'm going with these. Be mindful of who is in your life and what you allow to be said and done around you. No negativity means no drama...and that's a great head start towards living a life of joy.

No Negativity Poem

In the spaces provided below, write a poem about your life reflecting on the theme 'no negativity'. Use the first letter of the phrase to start each sentence:

Brave Act

N
O
N
E
G
A
T
I
V
I
T
Y

What does beautiful mean?

Beauty. A six-letter word, yet it has so much impact in society. This word has launched movements, defined entire generations and sent millions on a quest to chase after it. Unfortunately, this word has also been used to mislead generations of girls and women who have and continue to measure themselves against the ever-changing standards of what so-called "beauty" is.

I mean, what does "beautiful" mean anyway?? And by the way...who gets to decide what beauty is?? Like, give me a break already!! The standards of beauty have changed so much throughout history, and every decade or so, we see a new shift in beauty trends. At some point in our lives, we've all worried whether we're beautiful enough to be appreciated and loved. Here's a hint: **YOU ARE!! PERIOD**. Whether you're more on the "frumpy" side of things or an "insta baddie" . . . **YOU ARE BEAUTIFUL**.

Beauty is so much more than just skin deep. There are so many qualities that make someone beautiful, and believe it or not, only a few of them have to do with aesthetics. Proof? It's easy: How many girls do you know right now who look incredible on the outside but people don't want anything to do with them because their personality is just horrible? Their disgusting attitude actually makes them unattractive to people. I know a few girls like that. Looks aren't everything. Trust me.

Take all of that pressure off you, hon, and don't even begin to try to fit some made up standard of beauty. Set your own standard, make your own rules.

> *"Don't spend your life trying to fit in...Stand Out!"*

For fun, let's look at past standards of beauty and how they've changed drastically over the years:

ANCIENT GREECE
UNIBROWS & BLEACHED CURLS (USED VINEGAR)

HEIAN JAPAN
FLOOR-LENGTH HAIR & SHAVED EYEBROWS (PENCILED IN CLOSE TO HAIRLINE)

18TH CENTURY FRANCE
DOUBLE CHINS & POWDERED HAIR

THE ROARING 20'S
SLIM SILHOUETTE & BOBBED HAIR (KNOWN AS "FLAPPERS")

1960'S
BIG DOE EYES, HEAVY LASHES & SUPER SHORT CUTS

1980'S
BIG HAIR WITH TONS OF HAIRSPRAY & NEON MAKEUP

2000'S
SUPERMODEL-THIN AND SMOKEY EYES

2010'S
CURVY BODIES WITH LIP & BUTT FILLERS

Different standards of beauty

Girl listen, society & media will tell you that beauty is a bag full of Fenty, MAC, Kylie Cosmetics or Sephora makeup. So many instagram accounts, reality shows and YouTube channels try their best to convince you that appearances are everything. Nothing could be further from the truth. Beauty doesn't come from concealer, highlight or a brow kit. In fact, there are so many other ways to measure beauty in a person.

Here is a list of attributes that beautify a person more than makeup ever could. Check off the ones that apply to you:

ATTRIBUTES OF BEAUTY	I HAVE THIS	WORKING ON IT
Sense of Humor		
Compassion		
Confidence		
Great Personality		
Humanitarian		
Loving		
Creative Mind		
Kindness		
Humility		
Joyful		
Intelligence		

Draw a self portrait and highlight the features that you love the most about yourself.

Favorite Features _____

> *"Beauty is not in the face; beauty is a light in the heart."*
> **- KAHIL GIBRAN -**

BRAVE: THIS IS US

brave

[Chapter 9]
FAMILY RELATIONSHIPS

Home

"I grew up in Canada, which is the friendly neighbor to the U.S., in a city called Toronto." That's how I had to describe my home up until ten years ago for people. Now I just say that I live in the 6ix . . . home of Drake, Justin Bieber, Shawn Mendes, and NBA champions, the Toronto Raptors! Yeah, I'm kind of bragging on that last one.

I lived in a low-income area that we call "government housing," which meant block townhouses that surrounded a communal parkette that we all shared. It felt like a packed sardine in a can at times, except here, the sardines knew everyone's business.

As kids, we knew who was struggling the most, who didn't have a dad, whose parent or parents weren't home because they were working all the time. We even knew who had gotten a beating, because the walls were so thin. Those kids were always greeted with the awkward, "Hey . . . you ok?" when they finally came back out to play.

I wish that I could tell you that I had a great start and an ideal upbringing that led to my being a leader in my community with several awards for my work. I wish I could . . . but I can't. My start in life was anything but that. In fact, my life was filled with so much pain that what the drugs & alcohol couldn't drown out, thoughts of suicide did. My life went from bad to worse, way before it turned around for good.

It was right before that turning point that I had a choice to make:
Make that part in my life only a small chapter of my life story or stay stuck on repeat and make it the absolute end of my story. It doesn't matter how horrible your beginning, you don't have to repeat the stories of your past or those of your family.

Your destiny comes with a fresh new start, and you should choose it. That fresh start means an opportunity to succeed in ways that your family never did (overcoming drugs & addictions, rising above poverty, not being a teen mom, being university educated with a degree, etc.). Whether they've encouraged you along the way or not, you have hundreds of people connected to this organization who are cheering you on. And loudly too!! I hope you can feel it, my brave warrior girl <3.

Rewrite your story

Whatever your story has been so far, it does not have to end here. God has much better and greater things in store! There is a new chapter in your story, waiting to be written. Put down your pen of hurt, pain, anger, and shame and pick up a new pen of hope, love, healing, and joy!

Brave Act

What would that new world look like for you? Rewrite your story:

My old story

My new story

Families: the good, the bad, and the ugly

Here's a thought:
We can't choose our families but we can choose how to love our families.

For some of you reading this, your family has been supportive and kind as you've grown up (and that is such a blessing); but for some of you, it has been the exact opposite.

How does that affect you as you grow into adults? One of the biggest things is that, like a mirror, we become the reflection of what has been projected onto us. Think about a mirror for a second . . . Whatever object you put in front of it, it will reflect the exact mirror image of that object. That's very much like you and I. We are a reflection of what has been poured into us or done to us (e.g., the girl who has been told she's ugly or worthless all her life will struggle in those areas to see herself differently).

However, the awesome news is that we don't have to stay in that state or mindset permanently.

For me, it was encountering the pure, unconditional love of God that changed the way I saw myself. I began to understand how He sees me, and I started to walk in that truth. It was then that my broken heart healed and I began refusing the lies that had been told to me. Whatever that pivotal moment is for you, my hope and prayer is that you will know today that no matter what has been projected onto you, you will not be a reflection of your past.

Sometimes in our lives, the family we've been raised in is not healthy and has toxic elements that have damaged us in very deep ways. Remember, we can't choose our family but we can choose how to love them. It could be that loving them well right now means loving them from a distance, until things get better. Don't feel guilty about that. I've learned that sometimes we need distance from a situation so that either they become different people or we become healed in order to forgive and love them enough to move forward.

Families come in different forms. For a season, they can be your friends, a foster family, people in a group home, your church community, or mentors. If you are being poured into positively and you feel uplifted and supported, then that's a good place to be.

True family doesn't always have the same last name. Sometimes the strongest families are the ones you make.

Brave act: a letter to your family

Think about how you were raised, your experiences, what was said to you growing up. Depending on your upbringing, you will have many things to reflect on in this exercise.

Make this letter one of the following:
A letter of gratitude
A letter of forgiveness
A letter to those who hurt you

Once you've completed it, please find someone that you can share it with for accountability and support.

Dear,

Famous celebrities who grew up in foster care

Did you know the following celebrities grew up in foster homes? Think of this as another great example of how our past doesn't dictate our future!

P.S. If you don't recognize a name, have some fun looking them up and finding out more about their amazing life!

John Lennon
Steve Jobs
Marilyn Monroe
Eddie Murphy
Cher
Malcolm X
James Dean
Ice T
Victoria Rowell
Alonzo Mourning
Michael Oher
Dante Culpepper
Tiffany Haddish
Simone Biles
Seal
Faith Hill
Sylvester Stallone

Mentorship

> *"Show me a successful individual and I'll show you someone who had real positive influences in his or her life. I don't care what you do for a living if you do it well, I'm sure there was someone cheering you on or showing the way. A mentor."*
> **— DENZEL WASHINGTON —**

When I get asked about my journey of success, I always give credit where it's due. And that's to God and the mentors that I had in my life. I've been truly privileged to have people of influence pour into the areas of my life: personal, spiritual, and business. Having mentors has been the key to my maturity, my growth, and my development. A good mentor should offer you guidance, honest advice, support, and wisdom. And tons of encouragement.

Just like Ciara said, it's time to "level up!" One of the ways you can do that is by connecting with someone older who can help steer you through the tough decisions and give you advice when you truly need it. I call it them being a "lighthouse." Think about a lighthouse for a minute and its purpose. A lighthouse helps navigate ships by illuminating (shedding light) on what's in front of them, including any rocks they need to avoid. In life, we all have storms and rocks along the way that cause us to delay, fall back or even crash in life.

Wouldn't it be awesome to have someone to help you through the journey, someone to help you avoid those nasty rocks and wrecks simply by helping you make better, more informed decisions?

Here are a few benefits of having a mentor in your life:

They are a constant source of support and encouragement

They are a great source of motivation

They help you realize your potential

They help you identify your strengths and weaknesses

They help you to learn a tremendous amount about yourself

They provide wisdom & guidance to help you make good life decisions

They become someone you can be accountable to

They are a listening ear for whatever you're going through

They provide much-needed perspective

brave

Reflection

> "Life is too short for fake butter or fake people. I would rather have an enemy who admits that they hate me, than a friend who secretly puts me down."
>
> **- KAREN SALMANSOHN -**

> "She's a jellyfisher: You have a conversation with her that seems all nice and friendly, then you suddenly feel like you've been stung and you don't know where it came from."
>
> **- HELEN FIELDING, BRIDGET JONES -**

> "The friendships we keep can shape more than just the outcome of a situation, these individuals can actually shape who we are, and inevitably, who we become."
>
> **- ALEX AND ANI -**

Chapter Reflections

Chapter 2 Reflections

Chapter 3 Reflections

Chapter 4 Reflections

Chapter 5 Reflections

Chapter 6 Reflections

Chapter 7 Reflections

Chapter 8 Reflections

Chapter 9 Reflections